Contents

Introduction

This report provides a brief overview of the asset management industry and an analysis of how asset management firms and the activities in which they engage can introduce vulnerabilities that could pose, amplify, or transmit threats to financial stability.

The Financial Stability Oversight Council (the Council) decided to study the activities of asset management firms to better inform its analysis of whether—and how—to consider such firms for enhanced prudential standards and supervision under Section 113 of the Dodd-Frank Act.[1] The Council asked the Office of Financial Research (OFR), in collaboration with Council members, to provide data and analysis to inform this consideration. This study responds to that request by analyzing industry activities, describing the factors that make the industry and individual firms vulnerable to financial shocks, and considering the channels through which the industry could transmit risks across financial markets.

The U.S. asset management industry oversees the allocation of approximately $53 trillion in financial assets (see Figure 1). The industry is central to the allocation of financial assets on behalf of investors. By facilitating investment for a broad cross-section of individuals and institutions, discretionary asset management plays a key role in capital formation and credit intermediation, while spreading any gains or losses across a diverse population of market participants. The industry is marked by a high degree of innovation, with new products and technologies frequently reshaping the competitive landscape and changing the way that financial services are provided.

Asset management firms and the funds that they manage transact with other financial institutions to transfer risks, achieve price discovery, and invest capital globally through a variety of activities. Asset management activities include allocating assets and selecting securities, using a variety of investment strategies in registered and non-registered funds; enhancing returns with derivatives or leverage; and creating customized investment solutions for larger clients, primarily through so-called separate accounts.

These activities differ in important ways from commercial banking and insurance activities. Asset managers act primarily as agents: managing assets on behalf of clients as opposed to investing on the managers' behalf. Losses are borne by—and gains accrue to—clients rather than asset management firms. In contrast, commercial banks and insurance companies typically act as principals: accepting deposits with a liability of redemption at par and on demand, or assuming specified liabilities with respect to policy holders.

However, some types of asset management activities are similar to those provided by banks and other nonbank financial companies, and increasingly cut across the financial system in a variety of ways. For example, asset managers may create funds that can be close substitutes for the money-like liabilities created by banks; they engage in various forms of liquidity transformation, primarily, but not exclusively, through collective investment vehicles; and they provide liquidity to clients and to financial markets.

The diversity of these activities and the vulnerabilities they may create, either separately or in combination, has attracted attention to the potential implications of these activities for financial stability. Some activities highlighted in this report that could create vulnerabilities—if improperly managed or accompanied by the use of leverage, liquidity transformation, or funding mismatches—include risk-taking in separate accounts and reinvestment of cash collateral from securities lending.

---

1   FSOC (2012a), p. 21644.

Unfortunately, there are limitations to the data currently available to measure, analyze, and monitor asset management firms and their diverse activities, and to evaluate their implications for financial stability. These data gaps are not broadly recognized. Indeed, there is a spectrum of data availability among asset management activities. Mutual funds and other investment companies registered under the Investment Company Act of 1940 (1940 Act) publicly report data on their holdings; banks report aggregated data on collective investment funds in regulatory Call Reports; and regulators have recently begun to collect data regarding private funds and parallel accounts on Form PF, under a mandate included in the Dodd-Frank Act. However, data for separate accounts managed by U.S. asset managers are not reported publicly and their activities are less transparent than are those of registered funds. Such accounts, according to estimates below, include roughly two-fifths or more of total assets under management (AUM) in U.S. firms. Privately owned asset management firms, which include several of the largest in the U.S., do not disclose information comparable to the public financial reports filed by asset managers that are public companies or subsidiaries of public companies. Data on some activities—such as involvement in repo transactions and the reinvestment of cash collateral from securities lending—are incomplete, thereby limiting visibility into market practices.

Reflecting these issues, this report describes:

- the activities of asset management firms and the funds they manage;

- the key factors that make the industry vulnerable to shocks: (1) "reaching for yield" and herding behaviors; (2) redemption risk in collective investment vehicles; (3) leverage, which can amplify asset price movements and increase the potential for fire sales; and (4) firms as sources of risk;

- the key channels through which shocks can be transmitted: exposures across funds and firms and the impacts of fire sales; and

- the data available to measure those activities, vulnerabilities, and channels, and the nature of the gaps in those data.

The report does not focus on particular risks posed by money market funds. In November 2012, the Council released a detailed analysis of these funds and their risks, and the Securities and Exchange Commission (SEC) recently proposed additional reforms.[2] In addition, the activities and risks posed by hedge funds, private equity, and other private funds are not addressed in detail. Additional analysis will be conducted in conjunction with further analysis of data that these funds have begun to file on Form PF. The OFR, SEC, and Commodity Futures Trading Commission (CFTC) are currently evaluating these data for monitoring purposes.

---

2   FSOC (2012c); SEC (2013).

Industry Activities

Asset managers provide investment management services and ancillary services to clients as fiduciary agents. The diversity of clients' needs results in a wide variety of firm structures and business models, ranging from investment boutiques that focus on a single product or clientele to large, complex financial institutions that offer multiple services.

Many asset managers focus their investment strategies on a single asset class, such as equities or fixed income; examples include long-only equity mutual funds and municipal bond funds. Some focus on a style of investing within an asset class, such as large-capitalization growth or dividend-yielding U.S. equities. Other managers cover broad market areas, offering multiple strategies within a fund or family of funds, and provide custom "solution" investment services for clients.

The industry is highly competitive and, in some ways, highly concentrated. Economies of scale in portfolio management and administration, combined with index-based strategies, have increased industry concentration in recent years. The largest asset managers generally offer the most comprehensive, low-cost client solutions. At the end of 2012, the top five mutual fund complexes managed 49 percent ($6.6 trillion) of U.S. mutual fund assets, including 48 percent ($2.8 trillion) of equity funds and 53 percent ($1.7 trillion) of fixed income funds. The top 25 mutual fund complexes managed 74 percent ($9.9 trillion) of U.S. mutual fund assets, including 74 percent ($4.3 trillion) of equity funds and 75 percent ($2.5 trillion) of fixed-income funds.[3] Ten firms each have more than $1 trillion in global assets under management (AUM), including nine U.S.-based managers, as concentration in the sector has increased (see Figure 2). Higher concentrations could increase the market impact of firm-level risks, such as operational risk and investment risk, or increase the risk of fire sales.

This narrative makes clear that asset management firms have a diverse mix of businesses and business models, offer a broad variety of funds, and engage in many activities. This diversity suggests that asset management activities should be the analytical building blocks for understanding the industry. Such an approach permits the flexibility to analyze risks posed by firms (firm divisions, or firms as consolidated entities) or by industry market sectors by aggregating activities and assessing the interplay among them. Analyzing activities individually or in combination permits analysis of transmission channels for risks, as well as assessments of how industry or firm practices could amplify risks to financial markets, institutions, or funds.

Figures 1 through 3 provide an overview of the asset management industry and its firms and activities. Figure 1 illustrates broad categories of sources of investable assets and translates them into various types of investment vehicles through the managers that provide them. It is important to note that there is inherent double-counting in the figure due to cross-investing among managers and to the use of several data sources. Figure 2 provides estimates for the top 20 asset managers by AUM. The table illustrates that firms vary significantly in the extent of their unregistered investment management activities. Figure 3 illustrates for these firms their relationship with their parent companies. The figures underscore that most of the data available to analyze the industry relate to firms or funds, not to activities. This report proposes a framework for reconciling activities with firms and identifies the gaps in data that must be filled for that crosswalk.

---

3   Morningstar Direct.

Figure 1: Asset Management Industry Overview *(as of 12/31/2012)*

PRIVATE INVESTABLE ASSETS[1]
assets under management in billions

Registered Investment Advisers (RIAs)
$45,400[2]

Broker-Dealer Firms
(with RIA affiliates included above)
$1,642[2]

Source: SIFMA

Insurance Companies
$8,670[3]

Source: P&I/OFR

Bank Holding Companies
$16,008

Source: P&I/OFR

Defined Benefit Plan Sponsors
Private Pensions: $6,636
State and Local: $3,193
Federal Government: $1,582

Total: $11,412

Source: Haver Analytics

Foundations & Endowments
Foundations: $646
Endowments: $406

Total: $1,052

Sources: Foundation Center, 2012 NACUBO Commonfund Study of Endowments

ASSET MANAGERS[1]
assets under management in billions

Registered Investment Advisers

Separate Accounts[4]
$10,076

Mutual Funds[5]
$13,181

Source: P&I/OFR, Morningstar

Insurance Companies

Off-Balance Sheet Separate Accounts
$6,030

Insurance Separate Accounts[6]
$2,070

Source: P&I/OFR, NAIC

Bank Holding Companies & Banks

Separate Accounts
$10,377

Common & Collective Trust Funds[7]
$2,337

Source: P&I/OFR, Call Reports

Private Fund Firms Regulatory AUM[8]

Hedge Funds
$4,767

Private Equity Funds
$2,717

Other Private Funds
$2,293

Source: SEC Form ADV

Money Market Funds: $2,651
Taxable: $2,358
Tax-free: $293

Fixed-Income Funds: $3,313
Bonds: $3,061
Exchange-traded (ETFs): $252

Equity Funds: $6,044
U.S. & International: $5,104
ETFs: $940

Other Strategies: $1,173
Allocation: $873 | ETFs: $3
Alternative: $92 | ETFs: $36
Commodities: $51 | ETFs: $118

Short-Term Investment/ Cash Funds: $239

Fixed-Income Funds: $439
Taxable: $433
Tax-free: $6

Equity Funds: $1,354
U.S.: $748
International: $606

Other Strategies: $305
Stock/Bond Blend: $196
Specialty/Other: $109

---

[1] Figures include double-counting due to cross-investing among managers and multi-sourcing of data in construction of table.
[2] Includes all non-exempt registered investment advisers as reported on the SEC's Form ADV.
[3] Some insurance companies reporting data to Pensions & Investments (P&I) classify insurance separate accounts and other on-balance sheet assets as assets under management.
[4] Separate accounts estimated by deducting registered funds from total world-wide assets under management using P&I data.
[5] Mutual funds registered in the United States.
[6] Separate accounts managed by an insurance company, in which the assets are on the insurance company's balance sheet.
[7] Does not include state chartered limited purpose trust companies.
[8] Regulatory AUM refers to gross assets under management, without adjusting for leverage.

Figure 2: Top 20 Asset Managers by Assets Under Management *(as of 12/31/2012)*

	Asset Managers	Worldwide (WW) AUM $ in billions	WW Registered Funds AUM[1] $ in billions	Registered Funds AUM as % of WW AUM	WW Unregistered AUM[2] $ in billions	Unregistered AUM as % of WW AUM
1	BlackRock Inc.	$3,791.6	$2,114.8	55.8%	$1,676.8	44.2%
2	Vanguard Group Inc.	$2,215.2	$2,124.3	95.9%	$90.9	4.1%
3	State Street Global Advisors	$2,086.2	$608.8	29.2%	$1,477.4	70.8%
4	Fidelity Investments	$1,888.3	$1,436.3	76.1%	$452.0	23.9%
5	Pacific Investment Management Company LLC	$1,624.3	$1,054.1	64.9%	$570.2	35.1%
6	J.P. Morgan Asset Management	$1,426.4	$742.1	52.0%	$684.3	48.0%
7	BNY Mellon Asset Management	$1,385.9	$490.7	35.4%	$895.2	64.6%
8	Deutsche Asset & Wealth Management	$1,244.4	$298.1[3]	24.0%	$946.4	76.0%
9	Prudential Financial	$1,060.3	$273.1	25.8%	$787.2	74.2%
10	Capital Research & Management Company	$1,045.6	$1,045.6	100.0%	$0.0	0.0%
11	Amundi	$959.8	$363.0	37.8%	$596.8	62.2%
12	The Goldman Sachs Group Inc.	$854.0	$338.0	39.6%	$516.0	60.4%
13	Franklin Templeton Investments	$781.8	$617.2	79.0%	$164.6	21.0%
14	Northern Trust Global Investments	$758.9	$152.9	20.1%	$606.0	79.9%
15	Wellington Management Company LLP	$757.7	$395.0	52.1%	$362.7	47.9%
16	AXA Investment Managers	$729.8	$203.3	27.9%	$526.6	72.1%
17	Metlife Inc.	$721.3	$0.0	0.0%	$721.3	100.0%
18	Invesco	$687.7	$443.8	64.5%	$243.9	35.5%
19	Legg Mason Inc.	$648.9	$353.6	54.5%	$295.3	45.5%
20	UBS Global Asset Management	$634.2	$12.1	1.9%	$622.2	98.1%

[1] WW Registered Funds AUM determined by summing P&I data on each asset manager's worldwide AUM and ETF AUM.
[2] WW Unregistered AUM determined by subtracting WW Registered Funds AUM from Worldwide AUM.
[3] For 2012, Deutsche Asset & Wealth Management declined to respond to the survey question on its registered funds, according to P&I. Its worldwide mutual fund AUM was $298.05 billion in 2011.
Sources: P&I, OFR Analysis

Figure 3: Top 20 Asset Managers with Parent Company and Type

	Highest Level Asset Management Entity	Parent Company	Parent Entity Type
1	BlackRock Inc.	BlackRock Inc.	Domestic entity other
2	Vanguard Group Inc.	Vanguard Group Inc.	Non-deposit trust company - member
3	State Street Global Advisors	State Street Corp.	Domestic financial holding company
4	Fidelity Investments	Fidelity Management & Research LLC	Domestic entity other
5	Pacific Investment Management Company	Allianz Asset Management	Foreign insurance
6	J.P. Morgan Asset Management	JPMorgan Chase & Company	Domestic financial holding company
7	BNY Mellon Asset Management	Bank of New York Mellon Corp.	Domestic financial holding company
8	Deutsche Asset & Wealth Management	Deutsche Bank AG	Foreign financial holding company
9	Prudential Asset Management	Prudential Financial Inc.	Domestic entity other
10	Capital Research & Management Company	The Capital Group Cos. Inc.	Domestic entity other
11	Amundi	Credit Agricole S.A., Societe Generale	Foreign financial holding company
12	Goldman Sachs Asset Management	The Goldman Sachs Group Inc.	Domestic financial holding company
13	Franklin Templeton Investments	Franklin Resources Inc.	Domestic financial holding company
14	Northern Trust Global Investments	Northern Trust Corp.	Domestic financial holding company
15	Wellington Management	Wellington Management Company LLP	Registered investment adviser
16	AXA Investment Managers	AXA S.A.	Foreign insurance
17	Metlife Investment Management	MetLife Inc.	Domestic entity other
18	Invesco	Invesco Ltd.	Domestic entity other
19	Legg Mason Capital Management	Legg Mason Inc.	Registered investment adviser
20	UBS Global Asset Management	UBS AG	Foreign financial holding company

Note: Domestic entity other is a Federal Reserve System designation for any legal entity that is not a bank, bank branch, foreign bank, or bank holding company.
Sources: Federal Reserve, P&I, OFR Analysis

Activities can be divided into functions performed at the client or fund level and those performed at the firm level. Activities at the fund level include asset allocation and security selection, as well as the management of fund liquidity and leverage. Portfolio managers allocate assets and select portfolio holdings according to the guidelines prescribed by a fund's prospectus or a separate account's investment management agreement. Figure 4 outlines business lines by significant asset class for large domestic asset managers. Activities undertaken at the firm level include centralized trading (including securities trading, derivatives trading, securities lending, and repo transactions), risk management, market and securities research, and administrative functions. Interconnections between fund- and firm-level activities are extensive; most funds rely on their sponsors for core services, and fund managers are typically employees of the advisory firm.

Risk management practices and structures vary significantly among firms. For example, although all registered investment companies and investment advisers are required by SEC regulation to have chief compliance officers, not all asset managers have chief risk officers.[4] Regardless of the structure used, effective risk management is important for the management of operational limits, counterparty limits, and investment concentrations across funds and accounts.

Some firms adopt a core investment strategy and implement that strategy across multiple funds and accounts. In addition, firms may offer strategies that seek to hedge risks across asset classes; for example, so-called risk-parity or all-weather funds combine equity and levered, fixed-income portfolios to achieve risk parity across the two asset classes. Such strategies may also be offered through multiple channels. Other activities undertaken at the firm level may either help to manage risk or result in increased risk across the firm's activities, such as taking on leverage through unsecured borrowing, establishing and maintaining redemption lines of credit,[5] and managing proprietary investments.[6]

As described in the sections that follow, a certain combination of fund- and firm-level activities within a large, complex firm, or engagement by a significant number of asset managers in riskier activities, could pose, amplify, or transmit a threat to the financial system. These threats may be particularly acute when a small number of firms dominate a particular activity or fund offering. Connections between asset management activities and other market activities could contribute to the transmission or amplification of risks from one market sector to another, irrespective of whether those risks originated from asset managers. Activities aimed at boosting returns through leverage, such as the use of derivatives, reliance on borrowing, or other means discussed below, could contribute to system-wide leverage and risk transfer. Figure 5 illustrates the connections from activities to vulnerabilities and transmission channels.

---

4   Investment Advisers Act, Rule 206(4)-7. Banks typically use different titles for employees performing these functions.
5   A redemption line of credit, provided by the firm that sponsors a fund or by a third party such as a bank, offers funds the ability to borrow to cover investor redemptions. As such, redemption lines offer fund managers the flexibility to keep less cash on hand, creating potential liquidity risks in the event of a market decline.
6   Fund management firms often make proprietary investments, for example, in the form of seed capital to new funds, although these investments tend to be small relative to client assets under management.

Figure 4: Significant Asset Class Business Lines of Large Domestic Asset Managers *(as of 12/31/2012)*

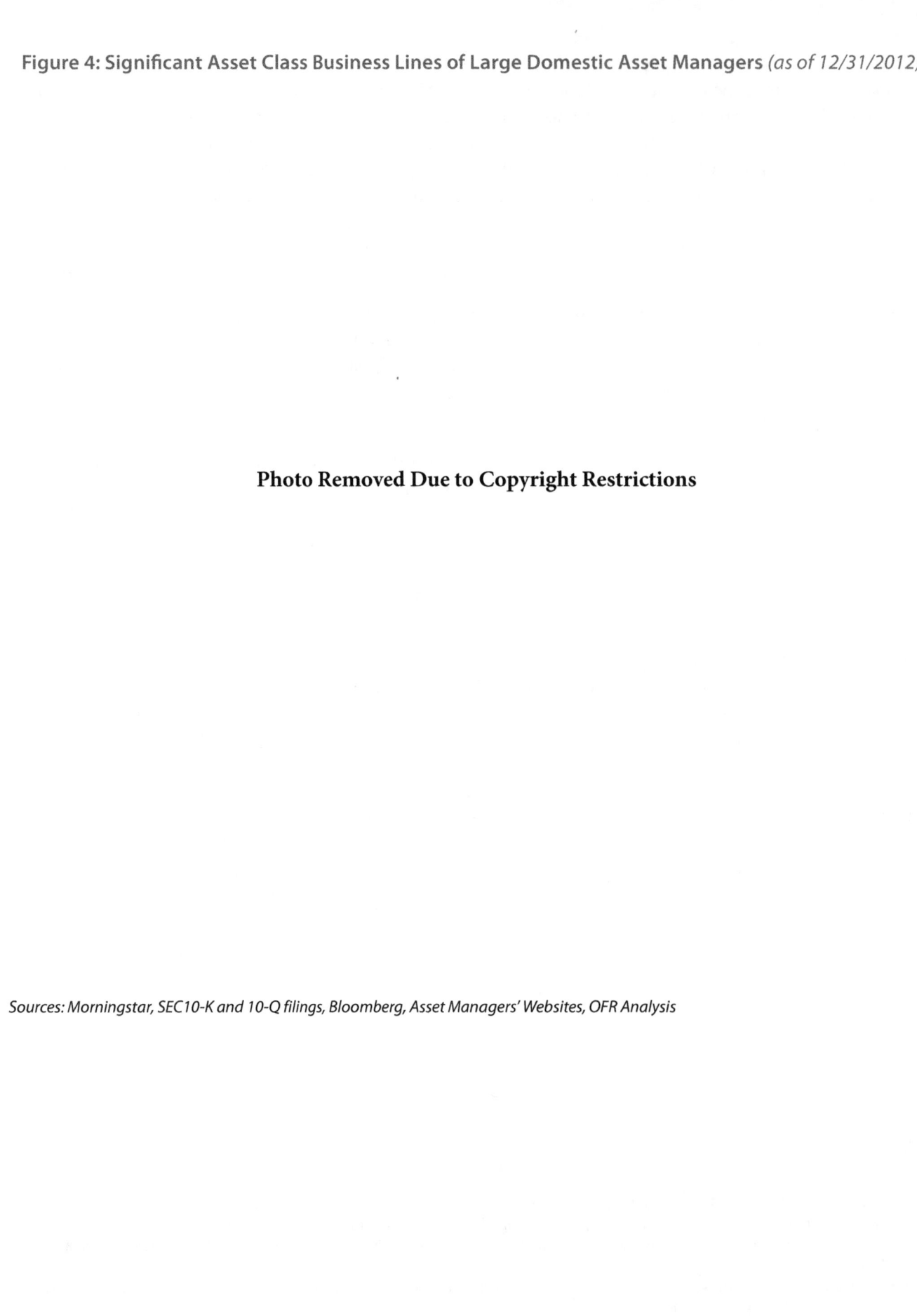

Photo Removed Due to Copyright Restrictions

Sources: Morningstar, SEC 10-K and 10-Q filings, Bloomberg, Asset Managers' Websites, OFR Analysis

Vulnerabilities

Factors that make the industry vulnerable to financial shocks include (1) "reaching for yield" and herding behaviors; (2) redemption risk in collective investment vehicles; (3) leverage, which can amplify asset price movements and increase the potential for fire sales; and (4) firms as sources of risk.

Reaching for yield and herding

An extended low interest rate investment climate, low market volatility, or competitive factors may lead some portfolio managers to "reach for yield," that is, seek higher returns by purchasing relatively riskier assets than they would otherwise for a particular investment strategy.[7] Some asset managers may also crowd or "herd" into popular asset classes or securities regardless of the size or liquidity of those asset classes or securities.[8] These behaviors could contribute to increases in asset prices, as well as magnify market volatility and distress if the markets, or particular market segments, face a sudden shock.

The asset management industry has many practices and regulatory restrictions that can mitigate such risks. For example, fund- and firm-level investment risk management is intended to ensure that investments conform to investment mandates and that credit quality, asset concentrations, volatility, leverage, and other issues are appropriately managed. Independent risk managers can reduce the risk of overextending portfolio mandates when they are empowered to challenge investment decisions.

Registered funds are required to disclose information to investors about their risks, portfolio holdings, concentrations, and investment strategies. Registered investment advisers are required to disclose to their clients in their annual brochures their significant investment strategies and related risks. In addition, regulatory restrictions are designed to align the interests of investment advisers and their clients and mitigate conflicts of interest. Managers have strong incentives to provide clients investment strategies matching their risk-return profiles. Given that most asset managers earn fees based on the amount of assets under management and that clients may freely move their accounts to another adviser or fund, advisers have strong incentives to meet client expectations.

However, potential information disparities between investment advisers and their clients could undermine those mitigants in the industry. Specifically, investors might not fully recognize or appreciate the nature of risks taken by their portfolio managers, despite required disclosures and investment mandate restrictions.[9] In some cases, managers' incentives (for example, some performance fees) may be structured so that managers share investors' gains on the upside but do not share investors' losses on the downside, a situation that creates incentives to invest in riskier assets.[10]

Competitive pressures may also increase incentives for managers to take on extra risks. For example, research on mutual funds has shown that managers who are lagging their peers toward year-end often take more risks than managers who are outperforming.[11] Depending on the flexibility of investment mandates, managers may take risks that investors do not fully appreciate. If these risks suddenly become apparent,

---

7   FSOC (2013), pp. 44-46, pp. 143-144; FSOC (2012b), pp. 139-141.
8   Wermers (1999); Sias (2004); Dasgupta, Prat, and Verardo (2011).
9   Spatt (2005).
10 Keane (2013); Huang, Sialm, and Zhang (2011).
11 Chevalier and Ellison (1997); Brown, Harlow, and Starks (1996).

they could spur redemptions and a flight to quality, which could in turn trigger adverse market contagion as managers sell assets to meet those redemptions.[12]

Regulation of asset managers often focuses on limiting conflicts of interest between asset managers and their clients, which can help mitigate these risks. However, such regulation focuses on helping ensure that managers adhere to their clients' desired risk-return profiles, but does not always address collective action problems and other broader behavioral issues that can contribute to asset price bubbles or other market cycles.

Figure 5: Asset Management Activities, Vulnerabilities, and Transmission Channels

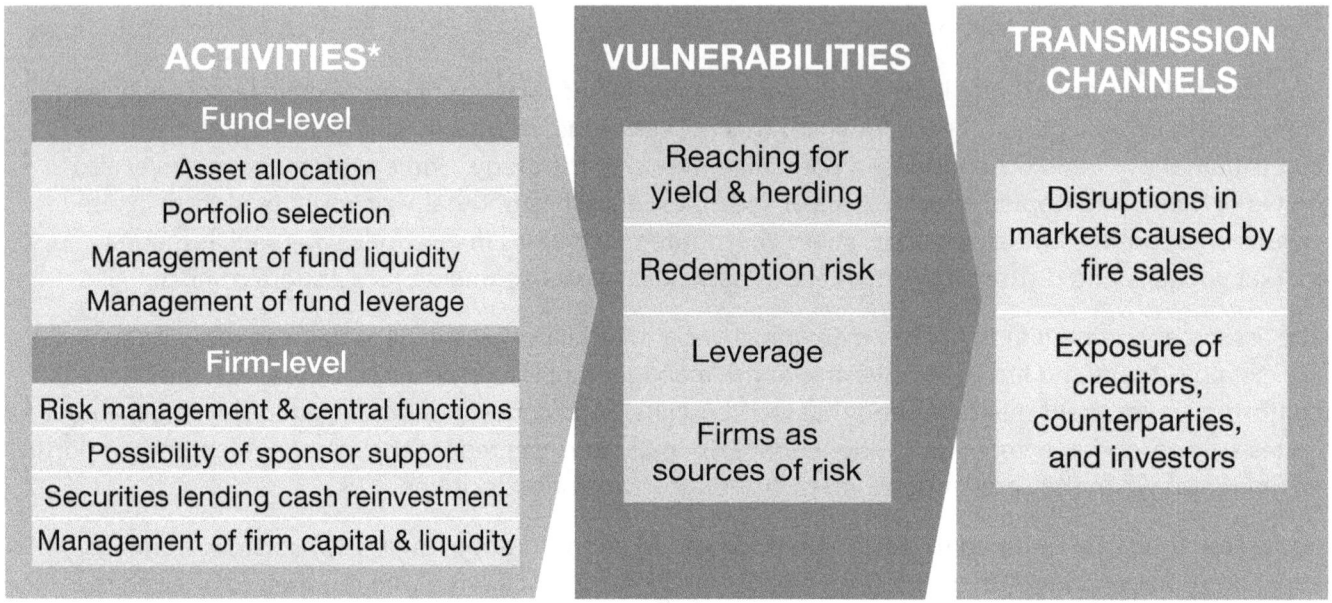

ACTIVITIES*

Fund-level

Asset allocation
Portfolio selection
Management of fund liquidity
Management of fund leverage

Firm-level

Risk management & central functions
Possibility of sponsor support
Securities lending cash reinvestment
Management of firm capital & liquidity

VULNERABILITIES

Reaching for yield & herding
Redemption risk
Leverage
Firms as sources of risk

TRANSMISSION CHANNELS

Disruptions in markets caused by fire sales
Exposure of creditors, counterparties, and investors

Example 1: Losses in highly leveraged funds, combined with reaching for yield behavior, could amplify fire sales and adversely affect fund counterparties.

Example 2: During a crisis, the rapid unwinding of investments of cash collateral from securities lending could pose risks that could amplify fire sales and trigger runs.*

* The activities and examples are illustrative and not exhaustive.

Competitive pressures can also be manifest in "herding"—the tendency of asset managers to crowd into similar, or even the same, assets at the same time. Such herding investment behavior in liquid assets may be unlikely to amplify financial stability shocks. Yet, herding into more illiquid investments may have a greater potential to create adverse market impacts if financial shocks trigger a reversal of the herding behavior. This behavior may occur because those assets appear to offer the best returns relative to the risks, but in other cases may result from competitive incentives or product types.

These potential risks could materialize in several different asset management activities. Pooled investment vehicles can potentially create market volatility and more rapid price impacts due to herding behaviors regarding investments in less liquid assets or increased redemptions due to shifting investments as risk tolerances or perceptions change.

---

12 Gennaioli, Shleifer, and Vishny (2012).

For example, exchange traded funds (ETFs) may transmit or amplify financial shocks originating elsewhere.[13] These products have provided investors generally low-cost access to diversified investment portfolios and have grown rapidly, with $1.34 trillion in combined U.S. assets at the end of 2012, up from $102 billion in 2002.[14] Although the majority of ETF assets are invested in the very liquid equity market, ETFs also are used to obtain low-cost, diversified exposure to less liquid market segments, such as fixed-income securities, emerging market assets, and municipal bonds.[15] Low interest rates in recent years have contributed to the rapid growth in fixed-income ETFs, with assets growing from $57 billion at the end of 2008 to $252 billion at the end of 2012, although this product line is still relatively small compared to bond funds, which had over $3.1 trillion in assets at the end of 2012.[16]

The effects on market liquidity of trading in ETFs are ambiguous. On one hand, trading in ETF shares could improve price discovery in relatively illiquid markets by providing a market price for a portfolio whose underlying holdings are thinly traded. On the other hand, ETFs, like many pooled vehicles, could also potentially accelerate or amplify price movements in markets during market turbulence, thus reducing market liquidity. In such circumstances, market makers may step away from making markets because they do not have good and reliable pricing information regarding those underlying portfolio holdings.[17]

Volatility and tight markets also can have unexpected impacts on ETFs. For example, during market stress on June 20, 2013, an ETF authorized participant temporarily ceased transmitting redemption orders to various ETFs because the authorized participant had reached an internal net capital ceiling imposed by its corporate banking parent. During that same day, another ETF opted to redeem shares only in-kind (rather than make available a cash redemption option) because the transaction costs to redeem in cash had exceeded the costs that the ETF set for that day. In order to address the role that ETFs may potentially have in transmitting market stress going forward, it will be critical to study how the ETFs' capital markets service providers and partners (authorized participants and market makers) cope with market stress and volatility.

Another way that these risks could surface is by investors herding into certain new products, particularly if the products are relatively illiquid and investors fail to fully appreciate their risks under different market conditions.[18] In recent years, asset managers have developed registered funds that allow retail investors to gain exposure to certain alternative investment strategies more typically pursued by hedge funds. For example, certain hedge fund and private equity fund managers have introduced mutual funds that are managed using alternative strategies. Such funds can introduce more complex trading strategies and embedded leverage than traditional retail mutual funds do. During a market shock, when the risks become

---

13 ETFs combine features of a mutual fund, which can be purchased or redeemed at the end of each trading day at its NAV per share, with the intraday trading feature of a closed-end fund, whose shares trade throughout the trading day at market prices. Only financial institutions designated as "authorized participants" are permitted to purchase and redeem shares directly from the ETF, and they can do so only in large blocks (for example, 50,000 ETF shares) commonly called "creation units." To purchase shares from an ETF, an authorized participant assembles and deposits a designated basket of securities and cash with the fund in exchange for ETF shares. Once the authorized participant receives the ETF shares, it is free to sell the ETF shares in the secondary market to individual investors, institutions, or market makers in the ETF. The redemption process is the reverse of the creation process. An authorized participant buys a large block of ETF shares on the open market and delivers those shares to the fund. In return, the authorized participant receives a pre-defined basket of individual securities, or the cash equivalent. This "hybrid" structure creates an arbitrage opportunity that generally keeps the ETF's market price relatively close to the ETF's underlying value. Unlike in the case of mutual fund shares, other investors can purchase and sell ETF shares only in market transactions and cannot purchase or sell creation units.

14 Investment Company Institute (2013a).

15 In June 2013, ETFs invested in equities held $1.17 trillion in assets while fixed income ETFs held $244 billion in assets. Investment Company Institute (2013b).

16 Morningstar Direct.

17 The Flash Crash on May 6, 2010 demonstrated the role ETFs can play in transmitting price dislocations in a distressed market. During that event, two-thirds of the 21,000 trades cancelled were trades in exchange-traded products. A joint SEC-CFTC report noted that "many of the securities experiencing the most severe price dislocations on May 6 were equity-based ETFs." The report also noted the liquidity mismatch between ETFs and the underlying securities: "Sell pressure that overwhelms immediately-available near-inside liquidity is less likely to be 'caught' by resting orders farther from the mid-quote in an ETF versus an individual stock." SEC-CFTC (2010).

18 Gennaioli, Shleifer, and Vishny (2012).

more apparent, investors who failed to appreciate the risks of these investments could engage in heavy redemptions of these products, exacerbating the shock.

It is important to recognize that asset managers can also have a stabilizing effect on the market. For example, asset managers with the financial strength and liquidity to buy assets trading significantly below their intrinsic values potentially could help to stabilize declines in prices.

Redemption risk

Any collective investment vehicle offering unrestricted redemption rights could face the risk of large redemption requests in a stressed market if investors believe that they will gain an economic advantage by being the first to redeem.[19] Investors in mutual funds with portfolios of securities with varying levels of liquidity may have a "first-mover advantage" to sell early, if they believe cash on hand and maturing assets are insufficient to cover redemption requests and that more liquid assets may need to be sold to meet redemptions.[20] In a stressed market environment, this scenario could leave slower-to-redeem investors holding shares of an increasingly less liquid portfolio whose net asset value (NAV) may fall at an accelerating rate as market liquidity premiums rise. Asset sales in response to redemptions could also spread stress from certain types of portfolio assets to other portfolio assets and market segments.[21] Heightened redemptions from an asset manager's funds could increase market risks if there is a perception that the asset management firm itself is at risk of failure.

Fund managers use well-established liquidity management tools to manage and mitigate redemption risk. As a precaution against high demand for redemptions, funds often hold cash buffers and maintain liquidity lines of credit. To meet redemption requests, under SEC guidelines, registered mutual funds should hold at least 85 percent of their investments in assets that the fund manager believes could be sold at or near carrying value within seven days.[22] Funds may increase the proportion of the portfolio invested in more liquid securities if they anticipate market turbulence or another shock that could lead to heavier redemptions. Many funds also track their investor redemption behaviors and plan heavier portfolio liquidity around times when fund investors are more likely to redeem, such as when tax payments are due or in anticipation of year-end tax loss selling. Some large asset managers trade directly with other buy-side firms through "dark pool" exchanges, primarily as a means of seeking best execution, but also to guard against potential situations in which traditional third-party liquidity providers—particularly broker-dealers—are unable or unwilling to provide sufficient trade liquidity.

Registered funds have little ability to impose restrictions to prevent heavy redemptions in times of stress. Registered funds generally may not suspend investor redemptions, and must satisfy redemption requests within seven days. Many mutual funds disclose that they may pay back investors "in kind"—in securities rather than in cash—if they are under severe stress, although practical challenges have rendered this tool rarely used by funds, even in times of severe stress. Mutual funds generally would not be able to impose redemption fees to counter sudden heavy redemptions under existing regulations. In contrast, private funds are often structured to permit temporary suspensions of redemptions or the imposition of redemption fees or gates that limit redemptions in times of stress.

During normal market conditions, the availability of liquidity in capital markets allows managers to trade securities in response to varying investor fund flows. Institutional investors tend to have more predictable funding needs based on fixed expenditures or liabilities, facilitating liquidity management for institutional

---

19 Mitchell, Pedersen, and Pulvino (2007).
20 Chen, Goldstein, and Jiang (2010).
21 Manconi, Massa, and Yasuda (2012).
22 SEC (1992).

funds; on the other hand, they tend to be quicker than retail investors to pull their funds in a market down-turn and take larger investment stakes. Although some fund managers may focus on holding more liquid assets, such as large capitalization stocks with narrow bid-ask spreads traded on multiple exchanges, others may focus on holding assets that are much less liquid, for example, collateralized loan obligations, emerging market equities, or thinly-traded corporate fixed income securities. If the liquidity of those assets varies significantly, and that variation widens under stress, fund investors in less liquid funds may perceive first-mover advantages to liquidating assets ahead of other investors. During the financial crisis, sophisticated investors tended to react more quickly to deteriorating market conditions than did retail investors, redeeming shares from funds more quickly if they perceived liquidity shortfalls.[23]

Figure 6 illustrates characteristics that make collective investment vehicles more vulnerable to redemption risks. On the vertical axis, risks are heightened for funds focused on preserving investor principal stability—such as money market funds or short-term investment funds (STIFs)—that offer daily liquidity to their investors.[24] Runs on such short-term funds can be self-reinforcing, as investor redemptions further drive down prices, returns, and liquid assets in the fund—spurring more redemptions. If perceived to have broader market implications, runs on these funds or groups of funds could contribute to risks of widespread fire sales.

Figure 6: Investors' Liquidity and Stability Preferences

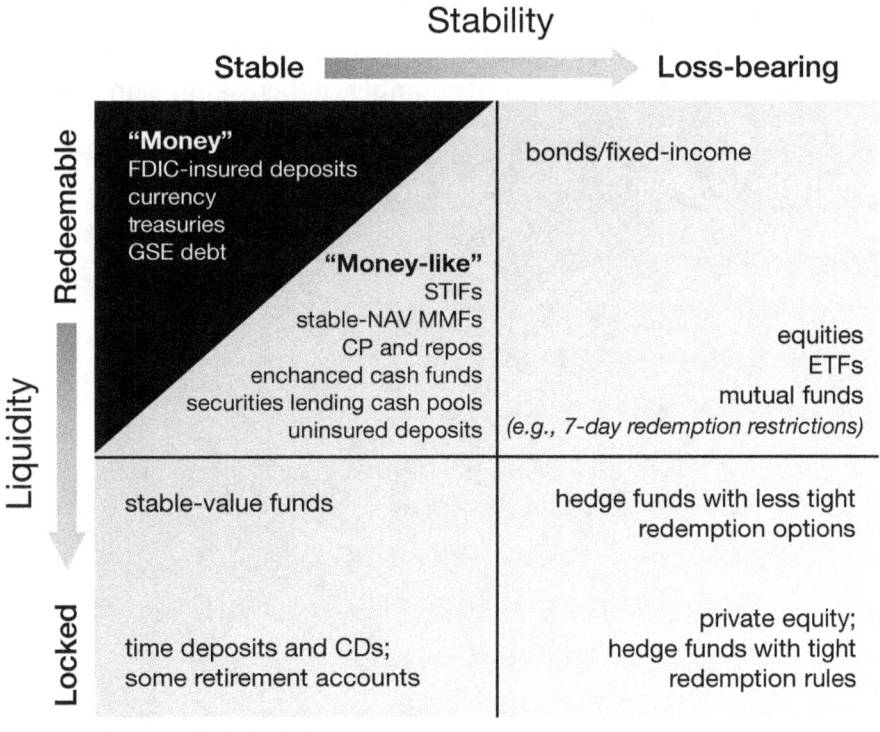

Source: OFR Analysis

Investors' concerns about the liquidity of one fund can quickly spread to similar or related funds, or to the sponsor of a fund complex. As an agency business, a financial services firm that suffers damage to its reputation through an extreme event in one business or fund may suffer redemptions or creditor pull-backs in its other funds or businesses. For example, investors in funds or accounts offered by a large asset

---

23 Schmidt, Timmermann, and Wermers (2013).

24 STIFs are a type of bank collective investment trust and are excluded from SEC registration and regulation under the 1940 Act; they are subject to rules established by banking regulators. The Office of the Comptroller of the Currency (OCC) introduced new rules to reduce risks in STIFs in 2012 (OCC, 2012). The SEC introduced new rules to reduce risks in money market mutual funds in 2010.

management fund complex may react negatively together if the family is tainted by an operational failure, exposure of poor risk management practices, or collapse of a single fund. Although firm-specific problems are often attributed to firm idiosyncrasies and may not have broader market impacts, problems associated with an activity involving a large number of asset managers could affect market confidence and lead to redemptions.

The horizontal axis of Figure 6 categorizes funds by investors' stability preferences. In some circumstances, investors may believe that they can rely on sponsor support of the fund or product in a crisis, even in the absence of a legal or stated guarantee. They may hold this belief because of the way a product was marketed or because such support has been granted in the past.[25] Although managers are not required to provide such support, competitive pressures or protecting firms' reputations may oblige it. Mutual funds and other types of products generally offer no guarantees that investors will be protected from principal loss, although many publicly-traded asset managers explicitly disclose in their regulatory filings (for example, Forms 10-K and 10-Q) that management reserves the right to provide support to any of their funds. In one example in November 2007, Bank of America supported investors in the $40 billion Strategic Cash Portfolio, then the largest enhanced cash fund in the country, and closed the fund after losses on mortgage-backed securities prompted the fund's largest investor to withdraw $20 billion.[26] In another example in November 2008, OppenheimerFunds contributed $150 million to a mutual fund to cover liquidity shortfalls due to derivatives exposures.[27] Direct and indirect support provided to investors in collective investment vehicles and separate accounts are not prominently disclosed, but, according to industry interviews, occurred during the crisis. Investors who expect their investments to be protected by explicit or implicit backstops could be expected to redeem funds in larger numbers if there is any sign that protections are eroding.

Figure 7: Net Worldwide Fund Flows, July 2008-June 2013 *($ in billions)*

There are other possible scenarios in which redemption risk could amplify financial or economic shocks. If a number of funds were invested in similar assets or correlated assets, market events affecting that strategy or

---

25 Brady, Anadu, and Cooper (2012).
26 Grynbaum (2007). Enhanced cash funds are short-term funds that seek to offer higher yields than typically achievable by money market funds.
27 SEC (2012).

set of assets may affect and cause heavier redemptions in a number of funds, and sales of assets from any of those funds could create contagion effects on the related funds, spreading and amplifying the shock and its market impacts.

For example, a significant amount of assets has flowed into fixed income and hybrid mutual funds in the past five years (see Figure 7). As of 2012, 32 percent of mutual funds were bond and hybrid funds. Bond funds could be exposed to a risk of sudden price declines if interest rates were to suddenly rise. In times of sharp changes in interest rates or related bond-market volatility, managers of these funds may be exposed to sudden heavier redemptions if they have not adequately managed the fund's liquidity, given market risks and the thinly traded nature of some fixed-income markets. Redemption risk is not prevalent in separate accounts because the assets are not managed in a collective investment vehicle. However, significant securities sales from separate accounts could still amplify a market impact.

Inadequate risk management relating to reinvestment of cash collateral for asset management securities lending programs illustrates how redemption-like risk can create contagion and amplify financial stability shocks. Lending available securities on an over-collateralized basis was considered a low-risk method to earn incremental income for a fund or separate account before the financial crisis. In a securities lending transaction, a security is temporarily transferred to a securities borrower, who may use it for short-selling, hedging, dividend arbitrage, or market-making.[28] Securities lenders often share revenues with agent lenders, who broker transactions, provide accounting services, manage transactions, and often reinvest the cash collateral. Most agent lenders also provide indemnity for any borrower default by paying the lender for any collateral deficiency.

Figure 8: Securities Lending Transaction Flowchart

Photo Removed due to copyright restrictions

Sources: Bank of England (2011), OFR Analysis

If securities lenders fear a loss of value in reinvested cash collateral due to market stress, they have an incentive to recall lent securities and exit reinvestment funds. Alternatively, borrowers may seek to return securities if they believe that their posted collateral may be at risk. The most prominent example during the crisis of inadequate risk management in cash collateral reinvestment occurred in the insurance context with

---

28   If the borrower of the security is a broker-dealer, it can only use the borrowed security for certain permitted purposes under Regulation T.

AIG. Through a subsidiary, AIG Securities Lending Corporation, AIG ran a large securities lending business on behalf of its life insurance subsidiaries. AIG Securities Lending Corporation's cash collateral reinvestment practices, coupled with AIG's financial distress, caused it to sell assets that had become illiquid at a loss in order to return the cash collateral. This substantially contributed to AIG's losses.

This risk was not limited to AIG. Some asset managers also invested cash collateral in assets adversely affected by the financial crisis, such as structured investment vehicles and Lehman Brothers notes, and they provided financial support to those cash collateral reinvestment funds.[29] The losses on cash collateral reinvestment amplified fire sales and runs during the crisis. They also contributed to the seizing of the money markets, in which cash collateral was typically invested. Daily marks and return of collateral due to the declining stock market further stressed the liquidity of collateral reinvestment funds.

Cash collateral reinvestment practices are not generally subject to comprehensive, targeted regulation and are not necessarily transparent to regulators or clients whose securities are lent. Due to data limitations, it is difficult to know, at any given time, the counterparty or risk exposures created by cash collateral reinvestment.

The connection between securities lending markets and cash collateral reinvestment, redemption risk, and short-term funding markets is not well understood and is difficult to measure due to a lack of comprehensive data.[30] When cash collateral is managed in separate accounts, visibility into these connections is reduced.

Figure 9: Percent of Securities Lending Loans by Industry *(as of 3/25/2013)*

Photo Removed due to Copyright Restrictions

---

29 For example, the Mount Vernon Securities Lending Prime Portfolio obtained an SEC staff no-action letter to enter into a capital support agreement with its affiliate due to its holdings of Lehman Brothers Holdings, Inc. notes and shares in the Reserve Primary Fund. SEC staff no-action letters relating to funds are available at http://www.sec.gov/divisions/investment.shtml.

30 Keane (2013).

Leverage

The recent crisis illustrated that leverage, particularly short-term leverage, can subject borrowers to margin calls and liquidity constraints that increase the risk of fire sales.[31] In addition to borrowing, asset managers obtain leverage for their funds and accounts through derivatives (futures, options, and swaps), securities lending, and repurchase agreements.

Investors can obtain leverage through products such as leveraged or derivative-based ETFs or other exchange-traded products that can magnify gains and losses for the investor compared to the underlying index or portfolio assets. Asset managers can use leverage at the firm level (borrowing by the firm itself), the fund level (fund borrowing, or closed-end funds offering both common and preferred shares), or the portfolio level (acquiring leveraged, structured products or trading in derivatives). Institutional investors and high-net-worth individuals face fewer limitations than smaller retail investors in obtaining leverage through managed funds and accounts. The Investment Company Act of 1940 (1940 Act) limits leverage levels for investment companies registered under that act. For example, mutual funds generally are required to hold assets equal to at least 300 percent of their bank debt, restricting leverage from bank debt to 33 percent of assets. Closed-end funds may also create leverage by issuing preferred shares.[32] However, unregistered funds and accounts are not subject to these regulatory restrictions.[33] Some complex trading strategies of such funds—such as "carry" trades in different currencies—often rely on leverage to boost returns.[34]

Registered funds also may incur additional leverage through the use of derivatives. Derivatives generally can create leverage by allowing funds to obtain exposure to market fluctuations in underlying reference assets—such as stock prices, commodity prices, or interest rates—that exceed the fund's investment in the derivative.[35] These transactions can either (1) result in the incurrence of potential debt obligations under the derivative contract, such as with a swap or future (indebtedness leverage), or (2) provide increased market exposure without the incurrence of future obligations, such as with a purchased option or structured note (economic leverage).[36] Registered funds are permitted to invest in derivatives, but are generally required to cover these positions with liquid assets equal to the indebtedness exposure created by the transaction; this cover requirement would either be the full obligation due at the end of the contract or, with respect to certain cash-settled derivatives, the daily mark-to-market liability, if any, of the fund under the derivative. Alternatively, a fund may be permitted to cover by holding an offsetting position that effectively eliminates the fund's exposure on the transaction. Cover is not required for instruments that create economic leverage but no indebtedness leverage.

Registered funds markedly expanded their exposure to credit derivatives in the run-up to the crisis. By 2008, 60 percent of the 100 largest U.S. corporate bond funds sold credit default swaps (CDS), up from 20 percent in 2004, according to a Federal Deposit Insurance Corporation working paper.[37] During the same period,

---

31 Brunnermeier and Pedersen (2009).
32 Closed-end funds can employ higher levels of leverage than mutual funds. Prior to the financial crisis, preferred shareholders in closed-end funds had a total of $64 billion in auction-rate preferred shares outstanding (Thomsen, 2008). These shares represented leverage for common shareholders. These shares were similar to auction-rate securities in that the interest rate was determined in periodic auctions. The freezing of the market for auction-rate securities in February 2008 affected auction-rate preferred shares issued by closed-end funds, increasing interest rates on the securities to default rates. Dividends on common shares fell significantly. Managers of closed-end funds used various means to support preferred shareholders without hurting common shareholders.
33 Although not subject to regulation, leverage levels for unregistered funds and accounts may be restricted under investment mandates.
34 A carry trade involves borrowing in a low-interest-rate market, typically a source of short-term wholesale funding, and investing the proceeds in (longer-term) higher-yielding assets, sometimes in a different currency from that of the sources of funding. For example, in recent years, investors borrowed in the U.S. dollar-denominated repo market to invest in foreign currency bonds.
35 Funds registered under the 1940 Act are required to submit semiannual disclosures of derivatives holdings to the SEC in Form N-Q, but more information would be required to analyze funds' derivatives exposures from a financial stability perspective.
36 SEC (1994), pp. 22-23.
37 Adam and Guettler (2010). In addition to seeking leverage, funds may invest in CDS to obtain exposure to issues that may be unavailable in cash markets.

the size of the average credit derivatives position in these funds grew from 2 percent to almost 14 percent, as measured by the notional value of the position relative to the fund's net asset value (NAV). The notional value exceeded 50 percent for six of the funds covered in the study. The study found that funds predominantly used CDS to increase their exposure to credit risks—that is, they were net sellers of credit protection, not net buyers.

During the financial crisis, the use of derivatives to boost leverage resulted in significant losses for some registered funds. For example, the Oppenheimer Champion Income Fund and Oppenheimer Core Bond Fund—two fixed-income retail mutual funds—lost roughly 80 percent and 36 percent of their NAV in 2008, respectively. The losses were primarily due to their exposure to total return swaps—a type of derivative in which investors exchange the total gains or losses from a reference asset without owning it—on AAA-rated tranched commercial mortgage-backed securities. OppenheimerFunds Inc., the funds' adviser, supported one of the funds that had insufficient liquidity to make payments related to margin calls on the risks associated with the swaps. The SEC later fined OppenheimerFunds $35 million for inadequately disclosing the risks associated with the leverage levels at the funds.[38]

In 2007, State Street paid significant settlements related to alleged fraudulent misrepresentations about the exposure of two funds to subprime mortgage credit risk and their use of leverage. The funds were leveraged approximately three-to-one through the use of total return swaps. These funds were unregistered collective investment funds managed by State Street Bank that targeted a stable NAV. Their leverage was unusually high for funds that were marketed as alternatives to money market funds, being more comparable to leverage employed at long/short hedge funds.[39]

The SEC issued a concept release in 2011 seeking public comment on the use of derivatives by registered funds. The release solicited comment on fund leverage, risk management practices, and derivatives exposure limits. Some of these potential options are similar to regulations recently implemented in Europe.[40]

As discussed below, data are currently insufficient to understand the exposures and the extent of leverage in separate accounts. As of earlier this year, Form PF requires all private funds to report data to the SEC related to their use of leverage.[41] The FSOC and the OFR have each noted the rationale and importance of monitoring leverage in the financial system in their annual reports to Congress.

Firms as sources of risk

The failure of a large asset management firm could be a source of risk, depending on its size, complexity, and the interaction among its various investment management strategies and activities. Distress at a large asset manager could amplify or transmit risks to other parts of the financial system. An asset manager's financial strength and reputation underpin its ability to attract clients, retain key employees, and deliver asset management services. Sponsors sometimes act in dual roles, as agents who provide portfolio management and other services, and as principals who may invest in their own funds or may provide implicit or explicit support to investors.

Concentration of risks among funds or activities within a firm may pose a threat to financial stability. Instability at a single asset manager could increase risks across the funds that it manages or across markets through its combination of activities.[42] In a variety of ways, firms' risk managers could fail to understand or

---

38 SEC (2012).
39 State Street was cited by the State of Massachusetts for noncompliance with state disclosure requirements.
40 SEC (2011); CESR (2010).
41 Certain private funds are required to report their secured and unsecured borrowings (for example, through loans or repos) as well as their use of derivatives. Analysis of these data will allow regulators to determine the overall use of leverage by private funds.
42 Bhattacharya, Lee, and Pool (2013); Gaspar, Massa, and Matos (2006).

anticipate risks with financial stability implications. For example, a firm could manage a number of large, highly leveraged unregistered funds which have strategies that turn out to be correlated in ways firm risk managers did not anticipate, either because correlations shifted in times of stress or because the manager failed to consider certain factors that led to correlations among portfolio assets.[43] Similar concerns could arise if a firm with extensive repo and securities lending businesses, and that managed strategies with an array of interconnections through derivatives and other exposures, had difficulty unwinding or transferring clients' investments to another asset manager during a period of market weakness. Under stress, counter-parties also might not distinguish among exposures to the firm and its funds, and therefore could take risk-mitigating actions that could aggravate risks across the firm's funds and accounts.

Interconnectedness and complexity can transmit or amplify threats to financial stability; large financial companies tend to have multiple business lines that are interconnected in complex ways. The asset management division of a bank or insurance company may be linked to other financial market segments directly or indirectly through business connections within the firm. For example, some large, dedicated asset management companies offer comprehensive services through in-house broker-dealers, commodity pool operators, trust companies, or captive insurance divisions. Some offer broker-dealer, consulting, or pricing services to other asset managers, creating interconnections and dependencies that increase their importance in financial markets. Some large asset managers also have subsidiaries in many countries, complicating risk management and increasing the difficulty of supervision.

Moreover, material distress at the firm level, or firm failure, could increase the likelihood and magnitude of redemptions from a firm's managed assets, possibly aggravating market contagion or contributing to a broader loss of confidence in markets. The largest asset managers continue to win a significant share of the market, primarily by offering comprehensive solutions that benefit from established franchises and economies of scale.[44] Although separate accounts are typically easy to move from manager to manager due to separation of custody and management, if an investment adviser managed a large amount of separate account assets with complex, highly-customized strategies, a new manager may not be willing or able to quickly replace an existing manager during a period of market turbulence, or clients may require managers to liquidate assets prior to a transfer contributing to market risk.

Several large, complex financial institutions with asset management divisions suffered material distress during the recent crisis. Recent policy measures that seek to reduce these risks include heightened prudential standards for banks and designated nonbank financial companies and enhanced resolution authorities. During the crisis, stress spread between these companies' other businesses and their asset management subsidiaries. Heightened redemptions from the funds and accounts managed by the asset management divisions of Bear Stearns, Wachovia, and Lehman occurred in step with other destabilizing events in the market.

As agency businesses, asset management companies tend to have small balance sheets, and nonbank, non-insurance asset managers are not required by U.S. regulation to set aside liquidity or capital reserves for their asset management businesses.[45] The Federal Reserve's annual stress test requires the asset management divisions of large bank holding companies with money-like funds to set aside capital to cover the risk that they would have to support some of their funds during stress conditions. Figure 10 shows the book value of large dedicated asset managers compared to their assets under management—one indication of

---

43 Boyson, Stahel, and Stulz (2010). Correlations typically rise in periods of stress, reducing the benefits of diversification.

44 The top 10 incumbent U.S. managers took 65 percent of all net new fund assets among managers with positive net flows in 2012 (BCG, 2013).

45 Nonbank fund managers in the United Kingdom are subject to prudential regulation and minimum capital requirements at the firm level. Those capital requirements are designed to cover emergency liquidity needs and are thus not comparable to regulatory capital requirements for banks and insurance companies (FSA, 2012).

available firm resources. These resources can be used for operational purposes, as well as to seed new funds or potentially provide sponsor support to funds based on market circumstances.[46]

Figure 10: Book Value of Listed Asset Managers

Photo Removed Due to Copyright Restrictions

Note: Data as of 4Q12, except if there is an asterisk.
* Data as of 3Q12.
** This is a Fitch rating.
^ Data estimated based on balance sheet (MMF AUM accounts for less than 1% of AUM).
Sources: S&P, SEC 10-K and 10-Q filings, Fitch, Moody's, OFR Analysis

---

46 Tangible book value excludes goodwill and other intangible assets in the calculation of assets. Negative tangible book value does not mean that a firm lacks cash or liquidity reserves.

Transmission Channels

Asset managers could transmit risks across the financial system through two primary channels: (1) Exposure of creditors, counterparties, investors, or other market participants to an asset manager or asset management activity, and (2) disruptions to financial markets caused by fire sales.

Exposure of creditors, counterparties, investors, or other market participants

The connections asset managers have with an array of financial companies, both within a holding company structure and with outside entities, could transmit risks among asset managers, other financial companies, and broader markets.

Direct connections among asset managers, banks, broker-dealers, insurance companies, and other financial services providers have grown over the past decade.[47] Banks and their subsidiaries are major service providers to the asset management industry, offering broker-dealer services, prime brokerage, fund accounting, custody services, and redemption lines of credit, as well as other forms of credit to funds and firms. Banks and insurance companies also serve as counterparties for various types of derivatives contracts and portfolio investments. Pricing providers offer valuation services enabling asset managers to mark their portfolios to market and calculate daily NAVs. Credit rating agencies also provide critical services. The extensive connections asset managers have with other financial services firms, and the concentration of some of these services, increase the potential that risks originating in other market sectors could be transmitted or amplified through asset managers into broader financial markets, or conversely, that risks originating in asset managers could be transmitted to other market sectors.

These industry linkages have increased the indirect connections among asset managers in recent years. Having common service providers, such as custodians, pricing providers, or securities lending brokers, or having common, large clients as investors, could result in common difficulties in the event of widespread service disruptions or redemptions. Fund-of-funds strategies that create implicit linkages between funds could also cause stress in the event of rapid redemptions, if severe price declines in more illiquid funds in the portfolio lead to increased selling pressure on more liquid funds.[48]

During interviews, asset managers suggested that counterparty risk management varies widely, with some firms establishing separate counterparty teams and others taking a fund-level approach subject to the discretion of portfolio managers. Funds are not specifically required to conduct ongoing credit analysis of their derivatives counterparties.

Disruptions to financial markets caused by fire sales

Fire sales are rapid sales of assets that temporarily depress market prices, typically reflecting market participants' responses to market distress, including an escalating premium on liquidity and demand for it.[49] Higher demand for liquidity associated with fire sales can magnify and spread quickly across both asset

---

47 Billio, Getmansky, Lo, and Pelizzon (2011).
48 Bhattacharya, Lee, and Pool (2013).
49 Begalle, Martin, McAndrews, and McLaughlin (2013).

classes and financial institutions, causing market prices to decline and market confidence to fall across market sectors.[50]

Fire sales can have a number of causes. Financial firms and market participants that use leverage or are required to maintain specific capital levels may be forced to sell assets at depressed prices if a decline in asset prices prompts higher haircuts or margin calls from creditors. Significant sales by a single large firm could depress asset valuation or increase market volatility, thereby transmitting stress to other institutions, which may then also face margin calls and be forced to sell assets, creating a knock-on effect. Alternatively, securities dealers having difficulty funding their activities may sell assets to generate liquidity, or investors in repurchase agreements may decide to sell collateral in the wake of a dealer default. Cascading effects from fire sales can amplify deterioration of market confidence and deepen a crisis.

In asset management, the following factors can increase the likelihood and severity of fire sales:

- **Large market positions and concentrations.** Fire sales may be exacerbated when a single fund or fund complex holds a large market position in a particular asset, sector, or strategy. This risk is heightened if the market has high informational or other barriers to entry; a lack of substitute investors could result in severe price depression if the fund or fund complex unwound its portfolio quickly. Asset managers managing large specialized funds and separate accounts with similar strategies may manage significant shares of important niche markets, which may not be fully transparent. Specialization concerns apply most directly to funds that focus on illiquid investments or funds that make large, concentrated bets.

- **Illiquid markets.** As markets become more illiquid, potentially due to market stress, they become increasingly prone to fire sales. Asset classes that tend to be less liquid include fixed-income securities, bank loans, and derivatives such as single-name credit default swaps. Customized or "bespoke" products can be particularly illiquid if they include complex combinations of derivatives and less liquid assets.

- **Reputation risk.** If an asset manager or one of its specialized funds suffers damage to its reputation, the redemption risk for the asset manager's funds could increase and heighten fire-sale risk. The potential asset pricing impact would be heightened if asset managers' funds and accounts held large positions in sectors with relatively low trading volumes, as in certain fixed income assets or markets.

- **Crowded trades.** Crowded trades can distort market prices and increase fire-sale risk. As discussed earlier, crowded trades occur when market participants have similar, correlated holdings in an asset class or trading strategy, and herding occurs. In the event of a shock, investors in crowded trades may try to sell or unwind their positions at the same time and in the same direction. Crowded trades may be especially problematic during a crisis, when few substitute investors may emerge to halt the downward spiral.

- **Leverage.** Excessive leverage can increase the risk that margin calls or other capital calls could prompt increased asset sales to cover positions. This risk is heightened in complex or less liquid funds, because price dislocation may be more severe, and during periods of market stress.

- **Transactions with liquidity "puts."** Certain transactions, such as securities lending and repo, have contractual obligations requiring liquidity upon demand and involve a large number of market

---

50   Coval and Stafford (2007); Jotikasthira, Lundblad, and Ramadorai (2012); Raddatz and Schmukler (2012).

participants. During periods of market stress, forced sales associated with these contractual obligations could increase the probability of fire sales.

- **Funding mismatches.** Short-term funding of long-term investments can lead to fire sales when funding liquidity is tight and investment values experience a negative shock.[51]

Mutual funds faced significant redemption requests during the crisis. According to Morningstar, redemptions from strategic income funds totaled $75 billion in the fourth quarter of 2008, nearly twice the volume during the quarter a year earlier, and redemptions by investors in government bond funds were $31 billion, 130 percent higher than during the fourth quarter of 2007. Although redemption risks that increase outflows from funds during periods of market stress do not necessarily pose threats themselves, they complicate liquidity management and can contribute to fire-sale risk.

According to some research, mutual funds in 2008 appeared to have been affected by fire-sale dynamics. Sharp declines in the value of their holdings of financial stocks may have compelled asset managers to sell off nonfinancial stocks in their portfolios as well. As evidence, researchers found in a 2012 paper that 10.5 percent of the 52 percent decline in the U.S. stock market related to the crisis could be attributed to distressed selling by mutual funds.[52] The paper noted, somewhat counter-intuitively, that this discount was highest for stocks that were considered stable and performed well before the crisis. In this way, funds sought to avoid realizing potentially large losses from selling stocks with the most depressed prices. Although this strategy had a stabilizing effect on the price of financial stocks, increased selling of nonfinancial stocks may have contributed to market weakness in other sectors.[53]

---

51 Boyson, Stahel, and Stulz (2010); Covitz, Liang, and Suarez (2013).
52 Hau and Lai (2012).
53 Manconi, Massa, and Yasuda (2012).

Data Gaps

Significant data gaps impede effective macroprudential analysis and oversight of asset management firms and activities. Data gaps block regulators' and supervisors' view of risk-taking, leverage, and liquidity transformation across financial markets and hinder their ability to fully analyze the nature and extent of financial stability risks relating to the asset management industry.

This section highlights several areas in which better data collection could facilitate macroprudential analysis, oversight, and monitoring of asset management firms and activities. Although increased data reporting requirements impose costs on firms, the OFR and regulators with jurisdiction over the firms and their activities discussed below could consider the extent to which significant benefits to financial stability monitoring could merit such increased reporting.

Data gaps in separate accounts

Registered investment advisers, banks, and insurance companies manage trillions of dollars in separate account assets; the top five asset management companies alone manage $5.5 trillion in separate accounts.[54] Data about the types of assets held in these accounts, their counterparty and other risk exposures, and amounts of leverage are limited. As a result, supervisors today are unable to fully assess the nature or extent of any financial stability risks that could be amplified or transmitted by the activities of these accounts.

In a separate account, an asset manager typically has discretion to select and manage assets on behalf of a large institutional investor or high net-worth individual under mandates defined in an investment management agreement (IMA). The client retains direct and sole ownership of the assets under management, which are typically held at an independent custodian on behalf of the client. Because separate accounts are not collective investment vehicles that pool together a variety of investors' assets (and thus, there is no shared risk or vulnerability to other shareholders' redemptions), separate accounts are not subject to restrictions under the 1940 Act, such as those relating to investment concentration or leverage. Rather, their ability to take on leverage or to invest in various asset classes or concentrated positions is specified in the IMA and thus is contractually agreed between the asset manager and the client.

In addition, advisers to separate accounts are regulated under the Investment Advisers Act of 1940, applicable bank fiduciary regulations, and applicable state investment adviser regulations (or other similar regulations). Private pension plans, which are often separate account clients, are required to abide by guidelines established by the Department of Labor under the Employee Retirement Income Security Act (ERISA). Although these regulators typically collect information about these advisers' assets under management, types of clients, and types of advisory activities, they do not routinely collect information about separate account holdings, leverage, risk exposures, or liquidity. In addition, although securities supervisors periodically examine asset managers that they regulate, including any separate accounts they manage, they

---

54 Insurer separate accounts, which include on-balance-sheet liabilities on the part of the offering insurance company, are not included in this analysis.

normally focus their examinations on ensuring that the manager adheres to fiduciary obligations, investor protection regulations, and contractual agreements such as the IMA.[55]

As a result of this regulatory framework, data to analyze aggregate exposures and asset holdings of separate accounts across asset management complexes are limited. Some private data providers gather data on separate accounts, but asset managers provide these data only on a voluntary basis and these data are inconsistent.

For a number of reasons, collecting additional data on leverage practices and risk exposures in separate accounts could be useful for financial stability monitoring. First, in some cases separate accounts are largely "clones" of existing strategies of funds managed by the asset manager, with small adjustments. Therefore, if the manager makes a shift in strategy in response to a financial shock, these clone accounts can magnify the impact of this strategy shift beyond the impact from its managed funds. Thus, separate accounts can potentially magnify the impacts from herding behavior.

In other cases, separate accounts can contain highly bespoke strategies that diverge significantly from registered fund strategies. For example, to generate higher returns for investors that would like to take on more risk than a pooled investment vehicle, a separate account manager might create a highly customized strategy involving illiquid securities or additional leverage.[56] These strategies can be idiosyncratic, and thus tend to diversify risk in the financial system and mitigate financial stability risks. However, if a number of large separate accounts take similar positions, particularly if highly leveraged or in a concentrated relatively illiquid market, those accounts could potentially help magnify or transmit financial stability shocks.

Given the limitations of existing data, the potential ways that separate account exposures or asset sales could affect markets are not adequately understood. Filling gaps in these data would allow for better macroprudential monitoring of related risks.

Data gaps in securities lending and repo markets

As noted earlier, monitoring the reinvestment of cash collateral from securities lending is important for financial stability purposes, but such monitoring is limited by a lack of data. Collecting transaction level and position data on securities lending between large international financial institutions, including the composition of the underlying cash collateral reinvestment assets, would improve regulators' visibility into market activities.[57] Section 984 of the Dodd-Frank Act requires the SEC to adopt rules increasing the transparency of information about securities lending available to broker-dealers and investors. Such a rulemaking could fill some of the data gaps described earlier.

Similar concerns exist regarding the involvement of asset managers in repo activity. During a period of market stress in which funding liquidity is drying up, firms with large repo books and an array of interconnections may have difficulty unwinding clients' investments quickly.[58] Because such a situation could dislocate markets and heighten fire-sale risk, data on repo activity are critical to monitoring developments that could indicate stress.[59] Currently, many repo transactions can be monitored only indirectly.[60] Although

---

55 National bank examinations of separate accounts focus on a bank's fiduciary duties to its customers, risks associated with the investment portfolios of these accounts, and the overall risks posed, in aggregate, by investment concentrations in these accounts and similarly run collective investment vehicles (OCC, 2001).

56 In one of our industry interviews, an asset manager noted that it was able to use separate accounts to replicate a hedge fund strategy that the manager did not offer to its fund investors.

57 Such an approach is consistent with the Financial Stability Board's Workstream 5 policy framework for addressing risks in repos and securities lending (FSB, 2012 and 2013).

58 FSOC (2013), pp. 133-134.

59 Begalle, Martin, McAndrews, and McLaughlin (2013); Martin, Skeie, and von Thadden (2012).

60 Tarullo (2013).

the SEC is considering approaches to enhance transparency in the closely related securities lending market, collecting data at the transaction level and position level on the overall volume of repo transactions in all three market segments—the tri-party, bilateral (that is, transactions settled between dealers on a delivery versus payment basis), and general collateral markets—would provide regulators a holistic view of asset managers, as well as interconnections and concentrations within repo markets.[61]

Data gaps at the firm level

Many of the largest asset managers are private and do not issue public financial statements. Assessing their financial positions and constructing a complete picture of their activities and interconnections is difficult, if not impossible. Lack of data on these firms limits the ability to assess their financial condition or identify activities, such as excessive borrowing or liquidity transformation, that could pose a threat to financial stability. Given that many large asset managers are private, cross-industry measurements of fundamental metrics, such as overall leverage, are difficult to calculate, which complicates effective macroprudential oversight.

Figure 11: Data Gaps

Data Gap	Data Currently Available	Data Required	Data Use
Private Companies	Some limited reviews by credit rating firms (some issue debt privately)	Financial statements of firms with standard notes	- Assess the financial standing of firms - Identify activities undertaken by firms
Separate Accounts	Self-reported aggregates with limited/inconsistent detail on strategies	Description of strategies and holdings	- Identify market concentrations by firm
Securities Lending	Market volumes and securities on loan	Data identifying beneficial owners lending activity	- Identify participants in market - Assess potential threat of material unwind in activity by fund and firm-lender concentrations
Repurchase Agreements	Volumes by firm settled at tri-party agents	Volume in bilateral settlement by fund/account	- Aggregate view of asset managers participation in market - Identify concentrations

---

61 Adrian, Begalle, Copeland, and Martin (2013) provide a template for needed data in both repo and securities lending; see also Bernanke (2013) and Tarullo (2012).

Appendix: Asset Management Firms and Activities

Firm types

Figure 1 displays the major participants in the asset management industry. Three kinds of firms are prominent:

- **Banks.** Banks often have asset management divisions through which they offer depositors and other customers' fiduciary services such as investment funds, wealth management services, trust services, and retirement products. These services may be offered through separate accounts or funds such as bank common trust funds or collective investment funds. A bank's investment management activities are exempt from SEC registration requirements unless the bank provides those services to an SEC-registered investment company, such as a mutual fund. In general, bank asset management activities are off-balance sheet.

- **Insurance companies.** Insurance companies often have asset management divisions that provide investment management and other services, such as retirement plans and guaranteed payments to clients. A number of insurance companies have acquired asset managers in recent years to expand their asset management businesses. For example, Allianz acquired PIMCO and AXA acquired AllianceBernstein. Insurance companies' asset management activities are distinct from their on-balance sheet insurance activities, such as those in their general accounts or associated with certain insurance separate accounts.

- **Dedicated asset management companies.** Dedicated asset management companies have two characteristics: (1) their main business is asset management, and (2) they are not integrated divisions of a bank or insurance company.[62] Although dedicated asset management companies are not regulated as bank holding companies by the Federal Reserve, many of them maintain a trust bank, regulated by the Office of the Comptroller of the Currency or a state bank regulatory agency, to offer collective investment funds to eligible clients or certain individual retirement account products, as required under ERISA. Several are very large organizations involved in disparate businesses, servicing many types of clients and offering services similar to those offered by banks. Some are publicly traded, while others are privately held and do not provide publicly available, consolidated financial statements. Most dedicated asset management companies are registered with, and regulated by, the SEC as investment advisers.

Fund types

There are four primary fund types in the industry:

- **Registered investment companies** are registered under the Investment Company Act of 1940 (1940 Act). They are required to abide by strict rules governing safekeeping and proper valuation of assets, transactions with affiliates, governance for fund management, use of leverage, and availability of

---

62 Some dedicated asset management companies are autonomous subsidiaries of large financial firms, such as PIMCO with respect to Allianz, and BlackRock with respect to PNC. The assets of these subsidiaries are generally not included on the parent firm's balance sheet and general management is delegated to the subsidiary.

liquidity, among other requirements. Registered investment companies include mutual funds, ETFs, closed-end funds, and unit investment trusts.

- **Private funds,** such as hedge funds and private equity funds, are excluded from registration under the 1940 Act, but advisers to these funds are generally required to register with the SEC or a state securities regulator.

- **Bank common and collective investment funds** are similarly excluded from rules under the 1940 Act, but, as noted earlier, are often subject to rules established by banking regulators.

- **Separate accounts** are accounts in which an asset manager selects assets on behalf of large institutional investors or high net-worth individuals under mandates defined in an investment management agreement. Clients retain direct and sole ownership of assets under management. Separate accounts are not specifically regulated under the 1940 Act, the Securities Act of 1933, or bank-specific regulations, although managers of those accounts are often registered investment advisers required to register with the SEC or a state securities regulator.[63]

---

63 Off-balance sheet separate accounts offered by asset managers differ from on-balance sheet separate accounts offered by insurance companies in that they generally do not have contracted manager liabilities. Insurance companies with asset management divisions often offer both asset management separate accounts (off-balance sheet) as well as insurance separate accounts (on-balance sheet).

References

Adam, Tim, and Andre Guettler. "The Use of Credit Default Swaps by U.S. Fixed-Income Mutual Funds." Working Paper No. 2011-01, Washington, D.C.: FDIC Center for Financial Research, November 19, 2010.

Adrian, Tobias, Brian Begalle, Adam Copeland, and Antoine Martin. "Repo and Securities Lending." Staff Report no. 529, New York: Federal Reserve Bank of New York, December 2011. Revised February 2013.

Bank of England. "Developments in the global securities lending market." Quarterly Bulletin 51, no. 3 (2011): 224-233.

Begalle, Brian J., Antoine Martin, James McAndrews, and Susan McLaughlin. "The Risk of Fire Sales in the Tri-Party Repo Market." Staff Report No. 616, New York: Federal Reserve Bank of New York, May 2013.

Bernanke, Ben S. "Monitoring the Financial System." Speech at the 49th Annual Conference on Bank Structure and Competition sponsored by the Federal Reserve Bank of Chicago, Chicago, May 10, 2013.

Bhattacharya, Utpal, Jung Hoon Lee, and Veronika Krepely Pool. "Conflicting Family Values in Mutual Fund Families." *Journal of Finance* 68, no. 1 (2013): 173-200.

Billio, Monica, Mila Getmansky, Andrew W. Lo, and Loriana Pelizzon. "Econometric Measures of Connectedness and Systemic Risk in the Finance and Insurance Sectors." MIT Sloan Research Paper No. 4774-10, Cambridge, Mass.: MIT, November 1, 2011.

The Boston Consulting Group. "Global Asset Management 2013: Capitalizing on the Recovery." Boston: BCG, 2013. https://www.bcgperspectives.com/content/articles/financial_institutions_ global_asset_management_2013_capitalizing_recovery/ (accessed July 12, 2013).

Boyson, Nicole, Christoff Stahel, and Rene Stulz. "Hedge Fund Contagion and Liquidity Shocks." *Journal of Finance* 65, no. 5 (2010): 1789-1816.

Brady, Steffanie, Ken Anadu, and Nathaniel Cooper. "The Stability of Prime Money Market Mutual Funds: Sponsor Support from 2007 to 2011." Working Paper RPA 12-3, Boston: Federal Reserve Bank of Boston, August 13, 2012.

Brown, Keith C., W. V. Harlow, and Laura T. Starks. "Of Tournaments and Temptations: An Analysis of Managerial Incentives in the Mutual Fund Industry." *Journal of Finance* 51, no. 1 (1996): 85-110.

Brunnermeier, Markus K., and Lasse H. Pedersen. "Market Liquidity and Funding Liquidity." *Review of Financial Studies* 22, no. 6 (2009): 2201-2238.

Chen, Qi, Itay Goldstein, and Wei Jiang. "Payoff Complementarities and Financial Fragility: Evidence from Mutual Fund Outflows." *Journal of Financial Economics* 97, (2010): 239-262.

Chevalier, Judith, and Glenn Ellison. "Risk Taking by Mutual Funds as a Response to Incentives." *Journal of Political Economy* 105, no. 6 (1997): 1167-1200.

Committee of European Securities Regulators. *CESR's Guidelines on Risk Measurement and the Calculation of Global Exposure and Counterparty Risk for UCITS.* Paris: CESR, July 28, 2010.

Coval, Joshua, and Erik Stafford. "Asset fire sales (and purchases) in equity markets." *Journal of Financial Economics* 86, no. 2 (2007): 479-512.

Covitz, Daniel, Nellie Liang, and Gustavo Suarez. "The Evolution of a Financial Crisis: Collapse of the Asset-Backed Commercial Paper Market." *Journal of Finance* 68, no. 3 (2013): 815-848.

Dasgupta, Amil, Andrea Prat, and Michela Verardo. "Institutional Trade Persistence and Long-Term Equity Returns." *Journal of Finance* 66, no. 2 (2011): 635-653.

Financial Services Authority. *Implementation of the Alternative Investment Fund Managers Directive.* Consultation Paper, London: FSA, November 14, 2012.

Financial Stability Board. *Strengthening Oversight and Regulation of Shadow Banking.* Consultative Document, FSB, November 18, 2012.

Financial Stability Board. *Strengthening Oversight and Regulation of Shadow Banking: Policy Framework for Addressing Shadow Banking Risks in Securities Lending and Repos and Policy Framework for Strengthening Oversight and Regulation of Shadow Banking Entities.* Consultative Documents, FSB, August 29, 2013.

Financial Stability Oversight Council. *Authority to Require Supervision and Regulation of Certain Nonbank Financial Companies.* Final Rule and Interpretive Guidance, Federal Register 77, no. 70, April 11. Washington, D.C.: FSOC, 2012a, 21637-21662.

Financial Stability Oversight Council. *2012 Annual Report.* Washington, D.C.: FSOC, 2012b.

Financial Stability Oversight Council. *Proposed Recommendations Regarding Money Market Mutual Fund Reform.* Washington, D.C.: FSOC, November 2012, 2012c.

Financial Stability Oversight Council. *2013 Annual Report.* Washington, D.C.: FSOC, 2013.

Gaspar, Jose-Miquel, Massimo Massa, and Pedro Matos. "Favoritism in Mutual Fund Families? Evidence on Strategic Cross-Fund Subsidiation." *Journal of Finance* 61, no. 1 (2006): 73-104.

Gennaioli, Nicola, Andrei Shleifer, and Robert Vishny. "Neglected Risks, Financial Innovation, and Financial Fragility." *Journal of Financial Economics* 104, no. 3 (2012): 453.

Grynbaum, Michael M. "Mortgage Crisis Forces the Closing of a Fund." *The New York Times,* December 11, 2007.

Hau, Harald, and Sandy Lai. "The Role of Equity Funds in the Financial Crisis Propagation." Research Paper No. 11-35, Geneva: Swiss Finance Institute, June 2, 2012.

Huang, Jennifer, Clemens Sialm, and Hanjiang Zhang. "Risk Shifting and Mutual Fund Performance." *Review of Financial Studies* 24, no. 8 (2011): 2515-2616.

Investment Company Institute. *2013 Investment Company Fact Book.* Washington, D.C.: ICI, 2013a.

Investment Company Institute. *Exchange-Traded Fund Data June 2013.* Washington, D.C.: ICI, 2013b.

Jotikasthira, Chotibhak, Christian Lundblad, and Tarun Ramadorai. "Asset Fire Sales and Purchases and the International Transmission of Funding Shocks." *Journal of Finance* 67, no. 6 (2012): 2015-2050.

Keane, Frank M. "Securities Loans Collateralized by Cash: Reinvestment Risk, Run Risk, and Incentive Issues." Federal Reserve Bank of New York, *Current Issues in Economics and Finance* 19, no. 3 (2013).

Manconi, Alberto, Massimo Massa, and Ayako Yasuda. "The Role of Institutional Investors in Propagating the Crisis of 2007–2008." *Journal of Financial Economics* 104, no. 3 (2012): 491-518.

Martin, Antoine, David Skeie, and Ernst-Ludwig von Thadden. "Repo Runs." Staff Report no. 444, New York: Federal Reserve Bank of New York, April 2010, Revised January 2012.

Mitchell, Mark, Lasse H. Pedersen, and Todd Pulvino. "Slow Moving Capital." *American Economic Review* 97, no. 2 (2007): 215-220.

Office of the Comptroller of the Currency. *Short-Term Investment Funds.* Final Rule, Federal Register 77, no. 70, October 9. Washington, D.C.: OCC, 2012, 61229-61238.

Office of the Comptroller of the Currency. *Comptroller's Handbook: Investment Management Services.* Washington, D.C.: OCC, 2001.

Raddatz, Claudio, and Sergio L. Schmukler. "On the International Transmission of Shocks: Micro-Evidence from Mutual Fund Portfolios." *Journal of International Economics* 88, no. 2 (2012): 357-374.

Schmidt, Lawrence D. W., Allan G. Timmermann, and Russ R. Wermers. "Runs on Money Market Mutual Funds." Working paper, January 2, 2013.

Securities and Exchange Commission. *Revisions of Guidelines to Form N-1A.* Investment Company Act Release No. 18612, Federal Register 57, No. 55, March 20, 1992. Washington, D.C.: SEC, 1992, 9828-9829.

Securities and Exchange Commission. *Mutual Funds and Derivative Instruments.* Division of Investment Management, September 26, 1994. Washington, D.C.: SEC, 1994.

Securities and Exchange Commission. *Use of Derivatives by Investment Companies under the Investment Company Act of 1940.* Concept Release, Federal Register 76, no. 173, September 7, 2011. Washington, D.C.: SEC, 2011, 55237-55255.

Securities and Exchange Commission. "OppenheimerFunds to Pay $35 Million to Settle SEC Charges for Misleading Statements during Financial Crisis." Press Release 2012-110, June 6, 2012. Washington, D.C.: SEC, 2012.

Securities and Exchange Commission. *Money Market Fund Reform.* Proposed Rule, Release No. 33-9408, IA-3616. Washington, D.C.: SEC, 2013.

Securities and Exchange Commission and Commodity Futures Trading Commission. *Findings Regarding the Market Events of May 6, 2010.* Washington, D.C.: SEC-CFTC, 2010. http://www.sec.gov/news/studies/2010/marketevents-report.pdf (accessed January 15, 2013).

Sias, Richard W. "Institutional Herding." *The Review of Financial Studies* 17, no. 1 (2004): 165-206.

Spatt, Chester S. "Conflicts of Interest in Asset Management." Speech at the Hedge Fund Regulation and Compliance Conference, New York, May 12, 2005.

Tarullo, Daniel K. "Shadow Banking After the Financial Crisis." Speech at the Federal Bank of San Francisco Conference on Challenges in Global Finance: The Role of Asia, San Francisco, June 12, 2012.

Tarullo, Daniel K. "Dodd-Frank Implementation." Testimony before the Committee on Banking, Housing, and Urban Affairs, U.S. Senate, Washington, D.C., July 11, 2013.

Thomsen, Linda C. "Testimony Concerning the SEC's Recent Actions With Respect to Auction Rate Securities." Testimony before the Committee on Financial Services, U.S. House of Representatives, Washington, D.C., September 18, 2008.

Wermers, Russ. "Mutual Fund Herding and the Impact on Stock Prices." *Journal of Finance 54,* no. 2 (1999): 581-622.

Office of Financial Research
U.S. Department of Treasury
www.treasury.gov/ofr

www.ingramcontent.com/pod-product-compliance
Lightning Source LLC
Chambersburg PA
CBHW080622180526

45168CB00007B/3022